Mysterious Encounters

Haunted Houses

by Kelli M. Brucken

KIDHAVEN PRESS

An imprint of Thomson Gale, a part of The Thomson Corporation

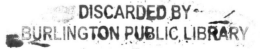

THOMSON
———*———™
GALE

Detroit • New York • San Francisco • San Diego • New Haven, Conn. • Waterville, Maine • London • Munich

Picture credits: © Joseph Paris, cover photo; Altrendo Images/Getty Images, 33; Archive Holdings Inc./Getty Images, 7; Barnaby Hall/Getty Images, 39; Ed Kashi/CORBIS, 41; Courtesy of Less EMF Inc., www.lessemf.com, 25; Fortean Picture Library, 11; Getty Images, 40; © Jessica Rinaldi/Reuters/CORBIS, 24, 30; © Joseph Paris, 5, 17; © Layne Kennedy/CORBIS, 18; © Lloyd Gerald, 14, 15; © Lloyd Gerald and Joseph Paris, 28; © Noah Voss, www.GetGhostGear.com, 27, 31; Paul Vozdic/Getty Images, 22; © Robert Holmes/CORBIS, 9; Stone/Getty Images, 21; The Image Bank/Getty Images, 35.

For more information, contact
KidHaven Press
27500 Drake Rd.
Farmington Hills, MI 48331-3535
Or you can visit our Internet site at http://www.gale.com

LIBRARY OF CONGRESS CATALOGING-IN-PUBLICATION DATA

Brucken, Kelli M., 1974-
  Haunted houses / by Kelli M. Brucken.
    p. cm. — (Mysterious Encounters)
  Includes bibliographical references and index.
  ISBN 0-7377-3475-2 (hard cover : alk. paper) 1. Haunted houses—Juvenile literature. I. Title. II. Series.
  BF1475.B78 2006
  131.1'22—dc22
                                                                        2005023418

Printed in the United States of America

Contents

Chapter 1
What Is a Haunted House?   4

Chapter 2
Houses Haunted by Tragedy   13

Chapter 3
Experiences of Haunted-House
   Investigators   23

Chapter 4
Dangerous Haunted Houses   32

Notes   42

Glossary   44

For Further Exploration   45

Index   47

Chapter 1

What Is a Haunted House?

In October 1976 Don Clancy, a college student at Kansas State University in Manhattan, Kansas, was studying in his room. Suddenly, his teeth started to chatter. He noticed his room had gotten incredibly cold.

Outside his closed window, he could hear footsteps crunching in the fallen leaves. That was not too odd, except it was after 1:00 A.M. He jumped up and looked out the window. No one was there. He went downstairs and outside to look around. He heard footsteps, even saw the imprint of a shoe as it smashed down on the leaves, but he saw no one.

Scared now, Clancy ran back upstairs to his room. After a few minutes he cracked his door open and

A glowing image appears in an upstairs window of an old house.

Creaks and Moans

Temperature changes can cause houses to shift slightly. To some people, the resulting creaks and moans might sound like the footsteps or cries of a ghost.

peeked out at the long hallway. The hallway was lined with doors that led to other bedrooms. What he saw amazed him. One after another, every doorknob on every door was slowly being turned. Clancy did not know it before, but it was clear to him now: He was living in a haunted house.

Haunted houses are believed to exist all over the world, in almost every town or community. Stories of hauntings have been told and recorded for centuries.

What Happens in a Haunted House?

A house is usually described as haunted when strange, unexplainable things happen in or around it. Some haunted houses have lights that turn on and off by themselves or doors that open and shut alone. Strong smells like smoke or perfume are sometimes noticed in haunted houses. These smells seem to come out of nowhere and fill an entire room, only to disappear as quickly as they came. Other unexplained occurrences in haunted houses include rocking chairs that rock by themselves, phantom footsteps, objects moved by unseen hands, or pets growling and staring at nothing. Some people hear voices in a haunted house, feel a cold touch by unseen fingers, or think someone is constantly watching them.

Types of Hauntings

Most people think haunted houses are haunted by **ghosts**. There are two different types of ghosts or hauntings that are believed to make a house haunted. The most common type is called a residual haunting.

A residual haunting is a play-back of past events. It is a bit like a videotape playing over and over again. The ghost involved is not an actual spirit. It is simply the im-age of a person, like the image of an actor on a movie screen.

A shadowy figure of a woman appears to walk through a room.

Experts believe a residual haunting may occur when someone does something over and over again in life, like walk down the same stairs and out the same front door at the same time every day. This repeated action leaves an energy behind that can be recorded or imprinted on a particular place.

Ghost experts think that this energy can be stored in a house's magnetic field. All houses contain a magnetic or electric field. This is an area around a power line, electrical wiring, or operating appliance in which the electric or magnetic current can be detected in the air. Ghost experts believe that over time this energy builds up until it is released. When this happens, it creates an image of the events that caused the energy.

Residual hauntings may be startling, but since no ghost is actually believed to be present, there is no chance that it can harm or communicate with the living. There is, however, another type of ghost that perhaps can.

Intelligent Haunting

When a ghost actually interacts with a person, it is called an intelligent ghost or haunting. In this type of haunting, the ghost is believed to know that it is a ghost. It is aware of its surroundings and can move around freely. Intelligent ghosts know when the living are present and, at times, even try to communicate with them.

An intelligent ghost is thought to be the spirit of a person that is trapped in the world of the living. For some reason, usually an untimely or tragic death, the spirit is unable to move on to the spirit world.

This type of ghost may choose to haunt a house for several reasons. The ghost may have lived in the house for a long time and resent anyone else living there. There may be some special object in the house that the ghost does not want to leave. Such a ghost may not even want to accept the fact that it is dead.

People who study ghosts say that almost any house potentially could be haunted. Ghosts tend to linger in places in which they once lived or in places where they died. All types of houses, whether they are big or small, old or new, could have a ghost living inside.

Famous Haunted Houses

Some houses are famous for being haunted. The Myrtles Plantation is a magnificent southern mansion located in St. Francisville, Louisiana. The house was

Empty rocking chairs await visitors on the porch of Louisiana's supposedly haunted Myrtles Plantation.

Who Was Harry Price?

Harry Price is one of England's most famous ghost hunters. In the 1930s and 1940s, no magazine, newspaper, or radio report on haunted houses was complete unless it had a contribution from Harry Price.

originally built for General David Bradford in 1796. It currently serves as an inn.

After author Frances Kermeen bought the Myrtles Plantation in 1980, she soon found out that it was haunted. Kermeen describes some of the ghosts she believes reside at the Myrtles in her book *Ghostly Encounters:*

> **Ethereal** parties keep guests awake until the wee hours. A servant carrying a candle makes her way from room to room at night, tucking in little boys and girls. A beautiful Indian maiden sits naked beside the pond. Two little girls, poisoned in 1824, romp and play outside, stopping occasionally to chat with an unsuspecting guest. The ruthless **overseer**, brutally murdered in the 1920s, confronts visitors and brusquely orders them away.[1]

The Myrtles Plantation has earned the name "America's Most Haunted House," given by the *Wall Street Journal,* because of its ghostly visitors.

The United States is not the only place with a famous haunted house. Borley Rectory in Essex, England, has long been believed to be haunted. Well-known ghost hunter Harry Price, who spent a year studying the house, describes it as "the most extraordinary and best documented case of haunting in the **annals** of physical research."[2] Price gave the house its nickname—the Most Haunted House in England—which was the title of a book he wrote in 1940.

Borley Rectory was built in 1863 by the Reverend Henry Bull, but events that happened on the same site many years before may be the cause of the rectory's hauntings. The most popular tale says that the site on which Borley Rectory sits was originally a **monastery**. Legend holds that a nun from a nearby convent fell in love with one of the monks.

England's Borley Rectory was said to be the scene of many bizarre happenings.

Borley Rectory a Fake?

Borley Rectory has long been considered the most haunted house in England. However, a new book by Louis Mayerling may end the rectory's reputation. Mayerling writes that he helped fake some 2,000 paranormal happenings in the house.

The two decided to run away together and get married. Before they could escape, they were caught. Their punishment was harsh. The monk was hanged, and the nun was buried alive inside the brick walls of the rectory. It is said that the two have haunted the location ever since.

Residents of Borley Rectory have reported pebbles that threw themselves, footsteps with no one about, lights being turned on by themselves, and objects disappearing. The ringing of bells, possessions being smashed to the floor, and people being yanked out of bed have also been reported. The figure of a ghostly nun has even been seen walking behind the rectory or peeking in the windows.

Are these houses really haunted by something from a **supernatural** world? No one knows for certain. Science has not been able to prove that haunted houses exist, but neither has it been able to prove that they do not.

Chapter 2

Houses Haunted by Tragedy

It is said that one of the most common reasons a spirit gets trapped in the world of the living is because of a traumatic, violent, or untimely death. That would explain why houses that have had tragedy occur in or near them seem quite often to be haunted.

The Whaley House

The Whaley House was built in 1857 in San Diego, California, for one of the first settlers of the area, Thomas Whaley. The house was constructed on a piece of land that was once the site of a gallows, a structure upon which people convicted of crimes were hanged.

Five years before the construction of the house, in 1852, a man known as "Yankee Jim" was convicted of trying to steal a boat and was hanged there. Some say the ghost of Yankee Jim never left the spot, even though the Whaley House was built right on top of it.

Whaley's youngest daughter, Lillian, was among the first people to report strange occurrences in the house. She lived in the home until her death in 1953 at age 89. She wrote in her **memoirs** that a force of some kind did not like her to go up to the second floor of the house.

Portraits of those who once lived in the Whaley House in San Diego, California, now adorn the walls.

Heavy footsteps heard upstairs haunted residents of the Whaley House.

She said the sound of heavy boots clomping upstairs was heard so often that she did not sleep well and was uncomfortable in her own home. Lillian was convinced it was Yankee Jim who paced in her upstairs rooms.

After Lillian Whaley died, no one lived in the house. It was scheduled to be torn down in 1956, but a group of citizens decided the house should be saved and kept open as a museum. June Reading was one of the citizens active in saving the house. She served as the museum director there for many years. She has had several encounters of her own with Yankee Jim.

On one occasion, Reading went upstairs with a fellow worker to investigate the sound of heavy footsteps. They looked everywhere but could find no evidence that anyone had been up there. They began to relax and walked over to a room called the nursery. Suddenly, the sound of a man's deep laugh came from right behind them. Reading recalled of the experience, "I knew that we had both heard laughter from the past. I felt what I can only describe as an intense electric shock go the length of my back, and for a few seconds I stood there frozen, truly unable to move. I have never had anything affect me in such a way."[3]

Has the spirit of Yankee Jim been residing in

Old Houses

Old houses have a reputation for being haunted. But are they really? In old houses, cold drafts often come through electrical outlets or light switches, furniture can slide on uneven floors, and squirrels or mice in attics can make weird noises.

A mysterious figure seems to hover near a doorway inside the Whaley House.

Whaley House ever since his hanging? Those who have heard his heavy pacing or deep laughter certainly believe so.

The Old Slave House

A house known as the Old Slave House, near Equality, Illinois, was the site of gruesome events in Illinois history. The house was built in 1842 by John Hart Crenshaw, a wealthy man. He was the owner of a huge salt-making operation that relied on

A ball and chain recall a time when slaves suffered horribly at the Old Slave House in Illinois.

the cheap labor of slaves he rented from slaveholders in Kentucky and Tennessee. As his thirst for wealth grew, Crenshaw began kidnapping slaves to work in his factory or to sell to other slaveholders.

Ghosts in the Attic

Black men, women, and children were said to have been smuggled into the house and held captive in jail cells built in the attic of Crenshaw's home. The cells were unheated, and slaves were chained to the floor. Torture devices and a whipping post were used to control the prisoners.

Crenshaw died in 1871. The house is now closed to the public, but for many years it was a museum. During that time, visitors often told stories of ghostly encounters in the haunted attic.

In the 1920s a man claiming to be an **exorcist** visited the Old Slave House. According to legend, the man was in perfect health when he went into the house but died a few hours later. George Sisk, a former owner of the house, thinks the man died of fright.

Thirty-five years after the exorcist's visit, two U.S. Marines were dared to spend the night in the attic of the house. Nothing happened until about one o'clock in the morning, when the light of their lamp began to flicker. A terrible moan shook the walls and mumbling voices filled the air. Ghostly forms hovered in the air just as the lamp went out, leaving the men in total darkness. The men retreated down the attic stairs, never to return.

George Sisk has stated that he does believe the house is haunted. Although he claims not to personally believe in ghosts, he says he does respect them.

The Story of David

Past tragedies can cause ghosts to haunt newer houses as well as historic ones like the Old Slave House. In 1990 an elderly couple purchased a house in Fresno, California. Although they knew someone had committed suicide inside the house, they were unaware his spirit was still lurking there.

As the couple settled in their new home, they did not notice much strange activity. Sometimes objects would go missing and turn up again in unusual places, but that was all.

One day, however, when the woman was alone in the house, she heard the unmistakable sound of someone whistling. She searched but found no one. From then on, the woman never felt completely alone in the house.

Cashing In on Ghosts

There are thousands of supposedly haunted inns and hotels around the world. It seems that having a ghost brings people from near and far. Skeptics believe it is not uncommon for owners to fake a ghost in order to cash in on tourist dollars.

A ghostly presence can show up anywhere, even in a bathroom, as one couple found.

Once the woman had just finished vacuuming her bathroom carpet. Her husband called to her a few minutes later to look at the floor. There, in front of the toilet, was the distinct impression of a man's shoe prints. They were too big to be her husband's, and he swore he had not set foot inside the bathroom.

A handprint on the couple's sliding glass door appeared next. The print was on the inside of the door

and had come from neither the woman nor her husband. The woman was disturbed by this as she kept imagining the lonely spirit pressed against the glass staring out into the outside world. She decided to call a priest into the home to see if he could help the spirit move on to the other side.

Could a restless spirit leave a handprint on a glass door? One couple thought so.

A short while after the priest had blessed the home, the woman awoke in the middle of the night. Something made her look toward her bedroom door. There she saw the shadowy figure of a man. The name "David" drifted through the woman's mind. As she stared at him, he slowly began to fade until finally there was only darkness. The woman felt that the ghost was leaving forever. She had a sense that he had come to say good-bye and perhaps to thank her for helping him move on.

Can a house that has been the scene of violence or tragedy be home to restless spirits? People who have had firsthand encounters with possible ghosts certainly think they can.

Chapter 3

Experiences of Haunted-House Investigators

Most people go out of their way to avoid an encounter with a haunted house. But certain individuals purposely seek out a house because it is haunted. These people are called ghost investigators.

The goal of ghost investigators or ghost hunters is to prove that life goes on after death. Special equipment, such as **electromagnetic field detectors**, digital photography, audio recording devices, and **thermal scanners**, helps these dedicated investigators

Investigators bang on a door in hopes of getting a reaction from ghosts at a supposedly haunted Rhode Island monastery.

find and document **paranormal** activity within a haunted house.

Ghost hunters have recorded experiences that they can describe in no other way but ghostly. Linda Zimmerman describes her experience this way: "I have heard footsteps and watched doors open, when no one was there. I have had icy cold masses of air engulf me, and felt the fear of being threatened by something I couldn't see. My cameras have captured objects that defy explanation.

You never know what to expect on [a ghost] investigation."[4]

The Boy Who Talked to Ghosts

The East Coast Ghost Hunters Club experienced an amazing event during one of its investigations. The club was called to a private home in Shokan, New York. The owners of the home wanted an investigation of the ghosts they believed were living in their home.

The first day the ghost hunters visited the home, they sat at a table talking with the family. On the table, the investigators placed their electromagnetic field detectors. The oldest son in the family, a seven-year-old, began talking to the detectors as if he could communicate with the ghosts through them. Suddenly, the detectors started beeping furiously.

The club had never experienced anything like this before. When the little boy asked the detector questions such as "What is your name?" the detector would go off. It would stop a few seconds later and remain quiet until the boy asked another question, when it would begin to beep again.

The investigators were amazed. This question-and-answer session lasted about 15 minutes. Then it stopped as suddenly as it had

An electromagnetic field detector is just one of the many tools used by people who investigate paranormal events.

started. Although club members took photographs during this weird activity, when they developed them, all of the photos appeared solid black, even though the flashes had gone off and three different cameras had been used. Other photos of the house taken during the same investigation turned out normal.

The East Coast Ghost Hunters Club was astonished. Its members told the homeowners that they believed the house was definitely haunted, but that the spirit was a nice one that watched over the children.

A Ghost in Colorado

Not all ghost investigators come across a spirit that is quite so friendly. In June 2002 the Rocky Mountain Paranormal Research Society in Colorado was called to investigate a mysterious presence in a family's home. The family's teenage daughter had been dabbling in witchcraft. Her parents believed she accidentally invited something from another world into their home.

When the club arrived at the home, members set up their equipment and started taking readings. Their machines picked up some sort of force near a pool table in the living room and another near a closet under the stairs.

During the night, the investigators heard a strange scratching noise around the closet area. They checked it out but could find no cause for the noise. The sound kept up in a fairly even pattern of scratching, pausing, then scratching again.

The investigators also saw ball-shaped lights called orbs. The orbs floated through the rooms, sometimes moving slowly and other times moving quickly. They even changed directions and hovered in certain spots. Two investigators also saw a dark form hovering near the ceiling, just outside the

Paranormal investigators believe that changes in a room's electromagnetic field are a sign that a ghost is present.

In an image created by an artist, glowing orbs appear to float above a cemetery at night.

closet. Throughout the night the team continued to see and sense weird things. One investigator reported being thumped in the head and feeling something toying with his shirt.

Around 5:00 A.M. the team brought the investigation to a close. Its general opinion was that the house was definitely haunted.

The Payne-Gentry House

Sometimes ghost hunters investigate famous haunted houses. In 2001 the Paranormal Activity Investigators of Kansas City, Missouri, visited a known haunted house, the Payne-Gentry House.

The Payne-Gentry House was built in 1870 for Elbridge and Mary Elizabeth Payne. In 1880 the Paynes's son, William, set up a medical practice in the lower level of the house. Local legend says that William experimented on patients in his office. In 1896 the Paynes's daughter, Mary Lee, lived in the house with her husband, William Gentry. Mary Lee died in the house giving birth to a daughter, who died as well.

Twenty-three ghosts have been reported as living in the house, which is now a museum. Visitors have reported unplugged lights turning on and red eyes or a face glowing in the attic window. A hangman's noose that suddenly disappears has been seen in a tree on the grounds of the house, and eerie laughter has been heard floating from the woods that surround the house.

During the 2001 investigation of the house by the Paranormal Activity Investigators, one team member

With compass and flashlight in hand, an investigator searches the dark woods around a supposedly haunted Rhode Island monastery.

noticed a swirling coldness around her lower legs. She measured the temperature of the air just below her knees and noticed it was ten degrees cooler than the rest of the air in the room. A psychic that accompanied the investigators remarked that the team member had a ghost dog sitting at her feet.

Another investigator felt a throbbing in her left hand at times. She had the feeling only in that one area of her body, and only in certain parts of the house. She also reported having to put a jacket on as she walked between two rooms. She says, "It felt like I walked into a refrigerator. I walked through a very large cold spot."[5] There were no air vents blowing cold air into that area, however, and the heat was on.

Icy Cold Air

Another investigator was especially drawn to the area of the house that had served as the doctor's office. She said she could feel energy that was left from pain and suffering that had taken place there. She also reported the feeling of someone giving the back of her jacket a strong tug. When she turned around, no one was there, but the air was icy cold. She says, "It chilled my hand to the bone, and it nearly felt like frostbite."[6]

Ghost hunters are true investigators who take their jobs seriously. They are searching the world for the indisputable evidence that life after death does exist, and they have had some ghostly encounters along the way.

An infrared digital thermometer with a laser sighting is one tool of the ghost-hunting trade.

Chapter 4

Dangerous Haunted Houses

Although living in a haunted house might be scary, haunting ghosts do not generally harm people. There are exceptions, however.

The Bell Witch

Between the years 1817 and 1821, the John Bell family of Tennessee was plagued by an angry ghost they called the Bell Witch. At first, a strange scratching sound was heard outside the house. Then, in 1818, the noises moved inside.

The family heard what they described as "a rat gnawing vigorously on the bed post."[7] But no rat was ever found. Soon, sheets and blankets were ripped from the family's beds. The horrifying sounds of something or someone choking and smacking its lips were heard, but nothing was ever seen.

John Bell Sr. began to suffer from strange illnesses. His tongue began to swell and feel stiff. Over time, his tongue became so swollen that it was hard for him to talk or eat. A voice screamed at John, saying it would torment him to death.

On the morning of December 19, 1820, the Bell family found John in a deep sleep, and they could not wake him. His son ran to get John's medicine, but the bottle was gone. Instead, there was a bottle of strange dark liquid. The ghost's

Bony hands reaching around the door frame of an old house suggest a scary, ghostly presence.

voice suddenly rang out: "It's useless for you to try to revive [him]. I have got him this time; he will never get up from that bed again. I put the [bottle] there, and gave [him] a big dose out of it last night while he was asleep, which fixed him."[8]

John Bell Sr. died the next day. This apparently pleased the ghost, as trouble from it slacked off afterward.

Was the Bell Witch a ghost? Was it so angry with John that its soul could not rest until it saw him dead? No one knows for sure, except possibly John Bell Sr. himself.

This Is My House

Sometimes, it appears that a ghost is angry because someone has moved into its house. That seemed to be the situation experienced by Marge and Ted Brower in Grand Rapids, Michigan.

One morning after the couple moved in, Ted got home from working the night shift. He found the attic door open and the light on. When he went to investigate, he noticed clothes strewn all over the floor. He called to Marge, who said she had not been in the attic at all. The Browers cleaned up the mess and locked the attic door.

For the next five days, they continued to find the attic open and objects tossed about the room. They found an expensive ladies' watch among the items. They had never seen the watch before and were not sure what to do with it. They decided to pack it away.

In many accounts of hauntings, ghostly images suddenly appear in stairwells.

The Mood for Ghosts

People who believe in ghosts may be more likely to see them. Experts say some people's bodies may have exaggerated responses to strange sounds and sights in places that are rumored to be haunted. This may convince them that they have experienced a ghost.

This seemed to end the attic episodes, and the house was peaceful. Marge and Ted began to relax. Then one night Marge heard the sound of claws raking at her bedroom window. The sound continued for several nights, and then something seemed to enter the house.

The couple heard heavy footsteps pacing upstairs. Ted closed the door to the stairway leading to the second floor of the house, but it had no lock. So he jammed butter knives into the doorjamb, to wedge the door closed.

That same night, Marge heard the heavy footsteps again. They came down the stairs and stopped at the closed door. Marge heard the knives being pulled out one by one. She ran to her bed and hid under the covers just as something opened the door. It clomped through the house and went out the back door.

Soon afterward weird noises began rising from the basement. When Ted went to investigate, one of the basement stairs collapsed under him. He almost fell onto the concrete floor but managed to catch himself. When he looked at the step, he noticed it had been cut in half with a saw.

Ted locked the basement door and shoved a solid oak table leaf under the doorknob. Surely, he thought, no one could get past that.

Just a week later, however, Marge heard faint noises coming from the basement. Then a terrible wailing floated up. It sounded like somebody in horrible pain. Just as suddenly as they had started, the wails stopped. Then slow, heavy footsteps began pacing up the basement stairs. A huge crash sounded as the table leaf split right down the middle. That was enough for Marge. She grabbed her coat and ran from the house.

The Back Bedroom

Ted and Marge moved out of the house, never to return. Perhaps that is what the ghost wanted all along. Bill and Lillian Adams certainly agree that a ghost can drive a family from a home, which is what happened to them in the early 1960s.

The Adamses were excited to move into their new home in Detroit, Michigan. Bill worked the night shift, and he decided that the small, dark bedroom at the back of the house would be perfect for him to sleep in during the day.

Things did not go smoothly, however. Bill had terrible nightmares the first time he slept in the room. He dreamed that he opened the closet and saw a hideous blood-soaked corpse. He woke up gagging, his body bathed in sweat.

He tried to forget the dreams, but they kept coming back. So he moved out of the room. Sleeping elsewhere seemed to take care of the problem, until Bill's mother visited in 1962.

A Horrible Smell

Since there were no other spare rooms, his mother settled into the bedroom at the back of the house. The very first night she complained of hearing weird noises. It was like someone was hammering on the closet door, trying to escape. Each night the sound returned, until the mother could no longer bear it and returned home.

Sometime later a friend of the family, Dick Patterson, visited. On Patterson's first night in the room, he woke up feeling as if someone had turned his body over in bed. He opened his eyes to see the figure of a woman.

Patterson jumped out of bed and raced toward the woman. Before he could reach her, all the lights went out. A few seconds later the lights came back on, but by then Patterson was in the kitchen with Lillian Adams.

Then a horrible smell drifted from the back room. The stench was so bad that it made Dick and Lillian feel sick. A terrible moaning started next, like someone was being killed. Terrified, Lillian called the police. When the officers arrived, they searched the house but found no one.

Bill decided he was going to find out once and for all who or what was in his house. The next evening he went to bed in the room. A few minutes later, he heard a shuffling sound outside the door. Thinking it was Lillian, he shouted for her to leave before she scared the ghost away.

Just then, he found himself looking into the most hideous face he had ever seen. Its eyes were empty and its mouth was making a strange hissing sound. A disgusting stench like sewage rolled from the figure's deformed body. Bill leaped from the bed and ran from the room.

Some people who have seen ghosts describe them as hideous and terrifying.

Within 24 hours the Adamses packed up their belongings and left the house. They did not know what was living in the back bedroom, but they decided it could keep the house.

From ghostly footsteps to evil actions, encounters with haunted houses have been reported by all

The Amityville Hoax

Amityville, New York, is home to one of the most famous haunted houses in America. Accounts of demons, green slime, and flying objects circulated until the 1970s when it was revealed that the owners had staged the hauntings trying to make a quick buck.

For many years, this house in Amityville, New York, was thought to be haunted.

The only way to tell whether this rundown house in Tennessee is haunted may be to spend the night there.

kinds of people. Could the mysteries of haunted houses be simple figments of the imagination? Or could they be something scarier? One may never know, until a night is spent in a haunted house!

Notes

Chapter 1: What Is a Haunted House?

1. Frances Kermeen, *Ghostly Encounters: True Stories of America's Inns and Hotels.* New York: Time Warner, 2002, pp. 5–6.
2. Quoted in "Borley Rectory Essex (1862– 1939)," Ghost Story, 2004. www.ghost story.co.uk/stories/borleyrectory.html.

Chapter 2: Houses Haunted by Tragedy

3. Quoted in Nancy Roberts, *Haunted Houses: Chilling Tales from 24 American Homes.* Guilford, CT: Globe Pequot, 1998, p. 30.

Chapter 3: Experiences of Haunted-House Investigators

4. Linda Zimmerman, "Haunted Highlights," 2004. www.ghostinvestigator.com/high lights/haunted_highlights.htm.
5. Quoted in Paranormal Activity Investigators, "Investigations," 2005. www.ghost-investigators. com/investigations/view_inv.php?inv_num=29.
6. Quoted in Paranormal Activity Investigators, "Investigations."

7. Quoted in Michael Norman, *Historic Haunted America*. New York: Time Warner, 1996, p. 457.
8. Quoted in Norman, *Historic Haunted America,* p. 459.

Glossary

annals: Historical records.

electromagnetic field detectors: Machines used to detect disruptions in the natural magnetic field.

ethereal: Something not of this world, or spiritual.

exorcist: Someone who believes he or she can free a spirit from the world of the living.

ghosts: Spirits of dead people that are trapped in the world of the living.

memoirs: A journal or book of a person's personal experiences.

monastery: A community of monks or other persons bound by religion.

overseer: One who keeps watch over, or directs the work of, others.

paranormal: Something beyond the range of normal experience.

supernatural: Something that is outside of the natural world.

thermal scanners: Machines used to measure the temperature of a room.

For Further Exploration

Books

Joan Holub, *The Haunted States of America*. New York: Aladdin Paperbacks, 2001. An exciting book filled with tales of spooky places and haunted houses in all 50 states.

Chris Oxlade, *The Mystery of Haunted Houses*. Des Plaines, IL: Heinemann Library, 2000. This book explores haunted houses and their ghosts. It offers theories to explain hauntings, including how they may be faked.

Jason Rich, *The Everything Ghost Book*. Avon, MA: Adams Media, 2001. This book is stuffed with spooky tales of haunted houses, spirits, ghost investigators, and unexplained mysteries.

Graham Watkins, *Ghosts and Poltergeists*. New York: Rosen, 2002. This book is packed with lots of amazing information about ghosts and poltergeists.

Web Sites

Ghost Haunts (www.ghosthaunts.com). A spooky site with ghost stories, haunted places, and great ghost links.

Ghost Hunters of St. Louis (www.stlghosts. com). This site is full of information on ghost hunting, ghost-hunting equipment, investigations, photos, and more.

Obiwan's UFO-Free Paranormal Page (www. ghosts.org). A great site with ghost stories, information on haunted houses across America, and ghost photos.

The Shadowlands (http://theshadowland.net/ ghost). This site is packed full of ghostly entertainment: ghost encounters, ghost-hunting education, famous hauntings, and a picture gallery

Index

Adams, Bill, 37–40
Adams, Lillian, 37–40
"America's Most Haunted House" (newspaper article), 10
Amityville, New York, 40

Bell family, 32–34
Bell Witch, 32–34
blessings, 22
Borley Rectory, 11–12
Bradford, David, 10
Brower, Marge, 34, 36–37
Brower, Ted, 34, 36–37
Bull, Henry, 11

Clancy, Don, 4, 6
Colorado, 26–28
Crenshaw, John Hart, 17, 19

David, 20–22
Detroit, Michigan, 37–40

East Coast Ghost Hunters Club, 25–26
electromagnetic fields, 8, 25–26
Equality, Illinois, 17, 19–20
Essex (England), 11–12
exorcism, 19, 22
explanations, scientific
electromagnetic fields, 8, 25–26
hoaxes, 12, 40

houses shifting, 6
in old houses, 16

footsteps, 4, 12, 16, 24, 36, 37
Fresno, California, 20–22

Gentry, Mary Lee, 29
Gentry, William, 29
ghost hunters/investigators
East Coast Ghost Hunters Club, 25–26
equipment used by, 23–24
goal of, 23
Harry Price, 10, 11
Paranormal Activity Investigators, 29–31
Rocky Mountain Paranormal Research Society, 26–28
Ghostly Encounters (Kermeen), 10
ghosts
intelligent hauntings and, 8–9
peripheral vision and, 26
residual hauntings and, 7–8
sightings of, 36, 38, 39
threats from, 33–34
Grand Rapids, Michigan, 34, 36–37

hoaxes, 12, 40

intelligent hauntings, 8–9

Kansas City, Missouri, 29–31
Kermeen, Frances, 10

laughter, 16, 29

Mayerling, Louis, 12
moans, 19, 38–39
Most Haunted House in
  England, 11
museums
  Old Slave House, 17, 19–20
  Payne-Gentry House, 29–31
  Whaley House, 13–17
Myrtles Plantation, 9–10

nightmares, 38
noises, 12, 16, 32–34
  footsteps, 4, 24, 36, 37
  laughter, 29
  moans, 19, 38–39
  pattern of, 27
  temperature changes and, 6
  whistling, 20

Old Slave House, 17, 19–20
orbs of light, 27

Paranormal Activity Investigators,
  29–31
Patterson, Dick, 38
Payne, Elbridge, 29
Payne, Mary Elizabeth, 29
Payne-Gentry House, 29–31
peripheral vision, 26
photographs, 26

Price, Harry, 10, 11

Reading, June, 16
residual hauntings, 7–8
Rocky Mountain Paranormal
  Research Society, 26–28

San Diego, California, 13–17
Shokan, New York, 25–26
side vision, 26
Sisk, George, 19, 20
slaves, 19
smells, 38, 39
St. Francisville, Louisiana,
  9–10

temperature changes
  coldness, 4, 24, 30–31
  from drafts, 16
  noises and, 6
Tennessee, 32–34
tourism, 20
types, of hauntings, 7–9

voices, 33–34

Wall Street Journal (newspaper),
  10
Whaley, Lillian, 14–15
Whaley, Thomas, 13
Whaley House, 13–17
whistling, 20
witchcraft, 26–27

Yankee Jim, 14, 15

Zimmerman, Linda, 24–25